PIANO • VOCAL • GUITAR

PIANO Bar hits

ISBN 978-1-4768-1606-7

HAL•LEONARD®
CORPORATION
7777 W. BLUEMOUND RD. P.O. BOX 13819 MILWAUKEE, WI 53213

ADDICTED TO LOVE

Words and Music by
ROBERT PALMER

Medium Rock

The lights are

on
signs
Instrumental

but you're not home:
but you can't read:

your
you're run-ning

mind
at

is not your
a dif-f'rent

BANG THE DRUM ALL DAY

Words and Music by
TODD RUNDGREN

AIN'T THAT A SHAME

Words and Music by ANTOINE DOMINO
and DAVE BARTHOLOMEW

AQUARIUS
from the Broadway Musical Production HAIR

Words by JAMES RADO and GEROME RAGNI
Music by GALT MacDERMOT

BILLIE JEAN

Written and Composed by
MICHAEL JACKSON

BLOWIN' IN THE WIND

Words and Music by
BOB DYLAN

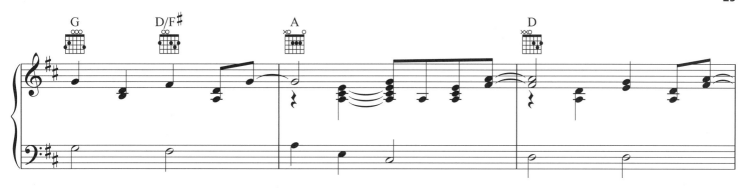

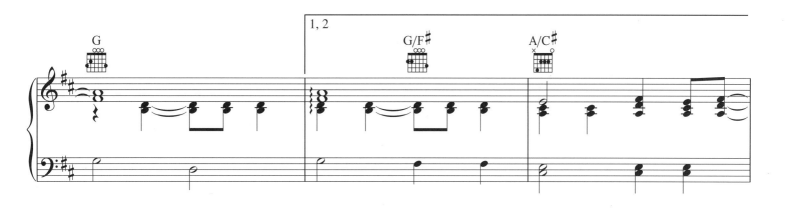

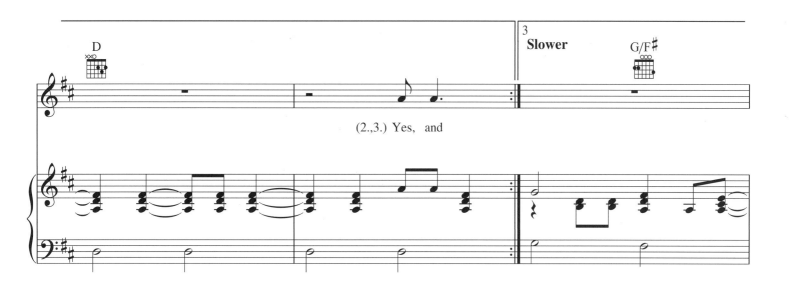

(2.,3.) Yes, and

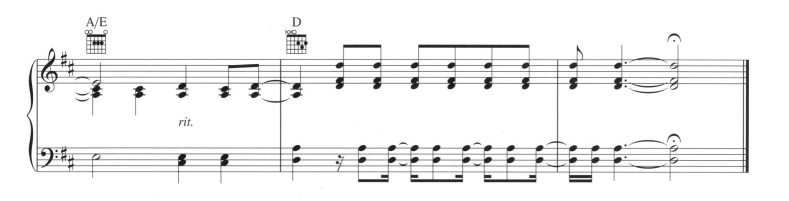

BUILD ME UP, BUTTERCUP

Words and Music by TONY MACAULAY
and MICHAEL D'ABO

say you will (say __ you will) but I love you still; __ I need you __ (I need you) __ more than an-

-y-one dar - ling you know that I have from the start. So

build me up (build __ me up) but - ter-cup don't break my heart.

To Coda ⊕

{ I'll be o - ver at ten, __ you tell me
{ To you I'm a toy __ but I could __

BYE BYE LOVE

Words and Music by FELICE BRYANT
and BOUDLEAUX BRYANT

CABARET
from the Musical CABARET

Words by FRED EBB
Music by JOHN KANDER

THE CANDY MAN

from WILLY WONKA AND THE CHOCOLATE FACTORY

Words and Music by LESLIE BRICUSSE
and ANTHONY NEWLEY

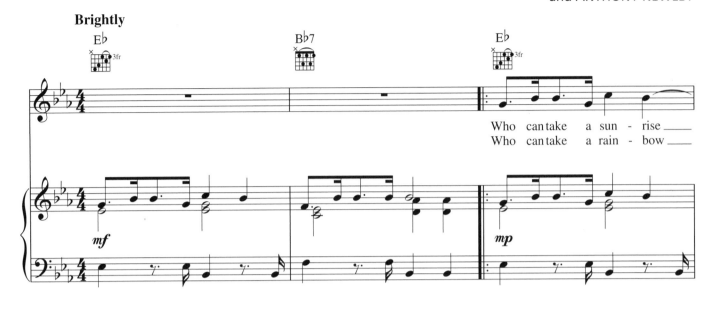

Brightly

Who can take a sun - rise ____
Who can take a rain - bow ____

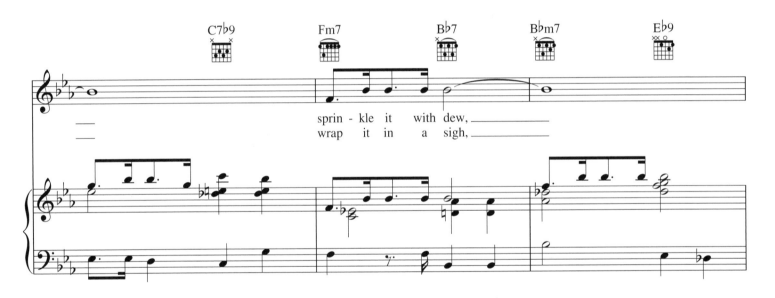

sprin - kle it with dew, ____
wrap it in a sigh, ____

cov - er it in choc - 'late and a mir - a - cle or two?)
soak it in the sun and make a straw - b'ry lem - on pie?)

The

CASEY JONES

Words by ROBERT HUNTER
Music by JERRY GARCIA

DING-DONG! THE WITCH IS DEAD

from THE WIZARD OF OZ

Lyric by E.Y. "YIP" HARBURG
Music by HAROLD ARLEN

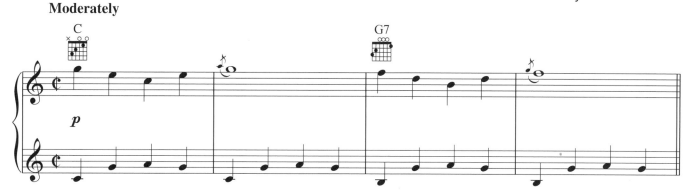

Once there was a wick-ed witch in the love-ly land of Oz, and a

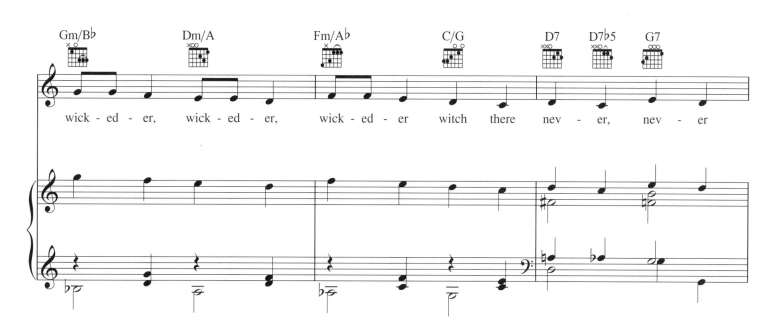

wick-ed-er, wick-ed-er, wick-ed-er witch there nev-er, nev-er

CLOSING TIME

Words and Music by
DAN WILSON

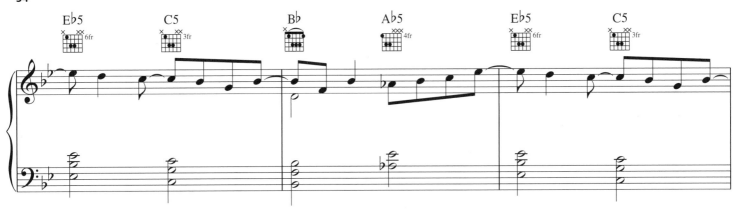

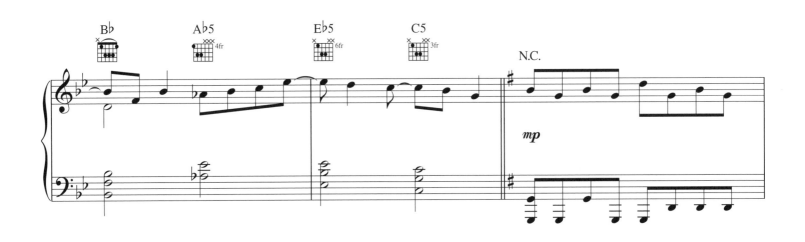

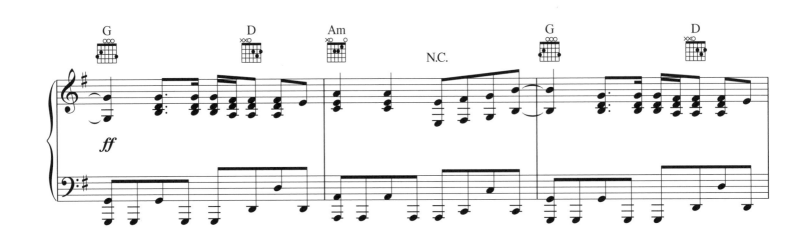

I know who __ I want __ to take me home. __

I know who __ I want __ to take me home, take me __

1

__ home. __

2

__ home. __

N.C.

Clos - ing time; __ ev - 'ry new be - gin - ning comes from

some oth - er be - gin - ning's end. __

DO-RE-MI
from THE SOUND OF MUSIC

Lyrics by OSCAR HAMMERSTEIN II
Music by RICHARD RODGERS

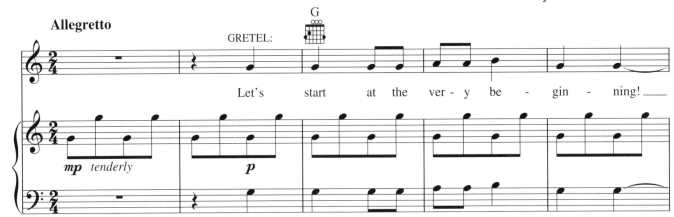

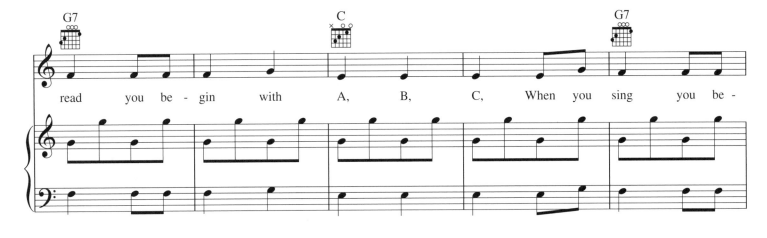

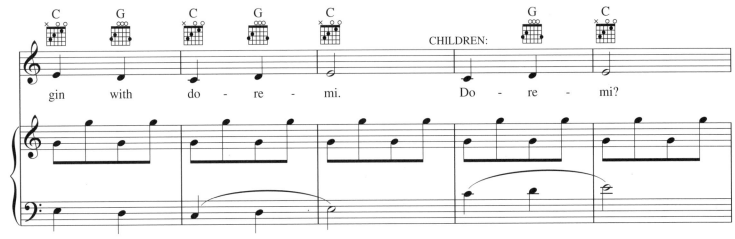

back to do - oh - oh - oh! (Guitar) A deer, a fe - male

deer, Do! (Guitar) A drop of gold - en sun, _____ Re!

(Guitar) A name I call my - self Mi! (Guitar) A

long, long way to run, _____ Fa! So! A nee - dle pull - ing

poco a poco cresc.

DON'T IT MAKE MY BROWN EYES BLUE

Words and Music by
RICHARD LEIGH

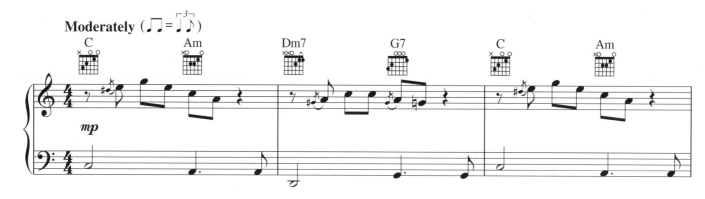

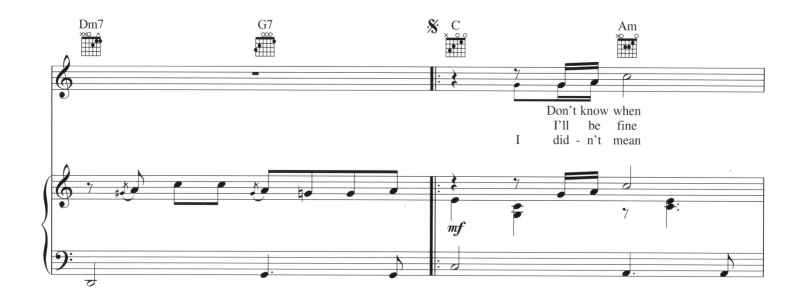

Don't know when
I'll be fine
I did-n't mean

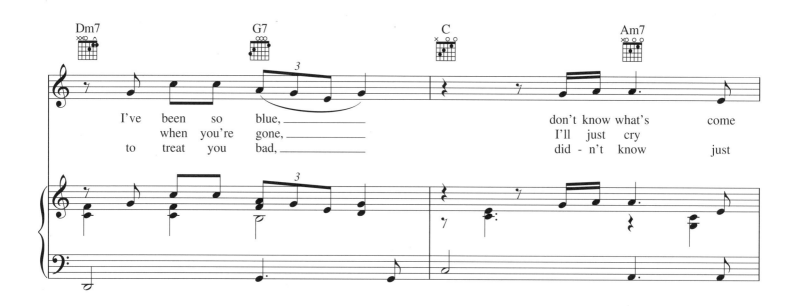

I've been so blue, _____ don't know what's come
when you're gone, _____ I'll just cry
to treat you bad, _____ did-n't know just

ESCAPE
(The Piña Colada Song)

Words and Music by
RUPERT HOLMES

Moderate groove

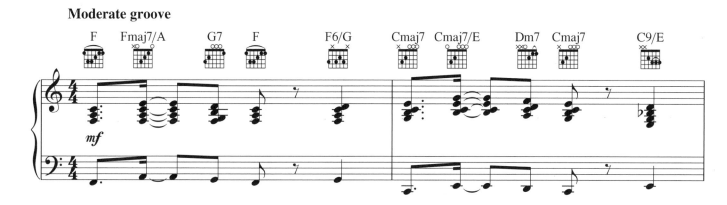

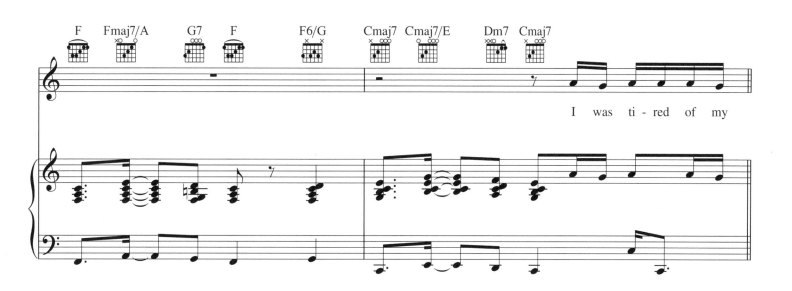

I was ti-red of my

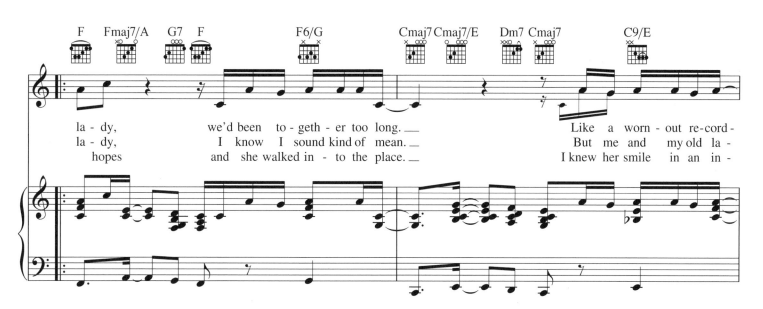

la - dy, we'd been to - geth - er too long. __ Like a worn - out re-cord-

la - dy, I know I sound kind of mean. __ But me and my old la -

hopes and she walked in - to the place. __ I knew her smile in an in -

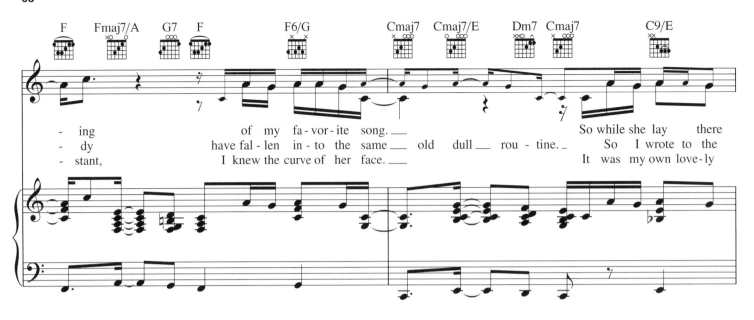

-ing / of my fa-vor-ite song. ___ So while she lay there
-dy / have fal-len in-to the same ___ old dull ___ rou-tine. _ So I wrote to the
-stant, / I knew the curve of her face. ___ It was my own love-ly

sleep-ing / I read the pa-per in bed. ___ And in the per-son-al col-
pa-per, / took out a per-son-al ad. ___ And though I'm no-bod-y's po-
la-dy, / and she said, "Oh, it's you." ___ Then we laughed for a mo-

-umns, / there was this let-ter I read: ___ If you like pi-ña co-
-et, / I thought it was-n't half bad. ___ Yes, I like pi-ña co-
-ment, / and I said, "I nev-er knew ___ that you liked pi-ña co-

la - das   and get - ting caught in the rain,   if you're not   in - to
la - das   and get - ting caught in the rain.   I'm not much in - to
la - das,   get - ting caught in the rain,   and the feel of the

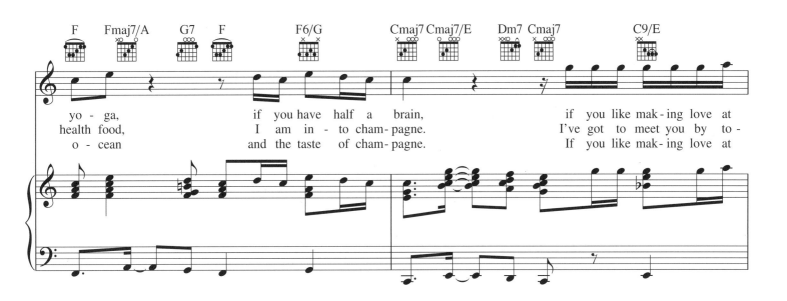

yo - ga,   if you have half a   brain,   if you like mak - ing love at
health food,   I am in - to cham - pagne.   I've got to meet you by to -
o - cean   and the taste of cham - pagne.   If you like mak - ing love at

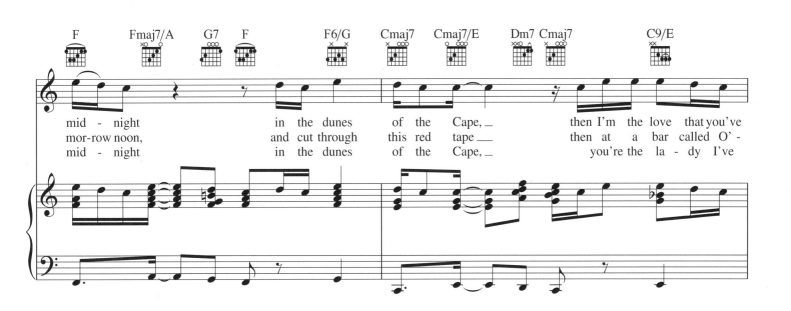

mid - night   in the dunes of the Cape, __   then I'm the love that you've
mor - row noon,   and cut through this red tape __   then at a   bar called O' -
mid - night   in the dunes of the Cape, __   you're the la - dy I've

looked for,   write to me   and   es - cape.
Mal - ley's   where we'll plan   our   es - cape.
looked for,   come with me   and   es - cape."

I did - n't think a - bout my
So I wait - ed with high

If you like pi - ña co - la - das   and get - ting caught in the

FOLSOM PRISON BLUES

Words and Music by
JOHN R. CASH

Additional Lyrics

3. I bet there's rich folks eatin' in a fancy dining car;
   They're prob'ly drinkin' coffee and smokin' big cigars.
   But I know I had it comin', I know I can't be free,
   But those people keep a-movin', and that's what tortures me.

4. Well, if they freed me from this prison, if that railroad train was mine,
   I bet I'd move on over a little farther down the line.
   Far from Folsom Prison, that's where I want to stay,
   And I'd let that lonesome whistle blow my blues away.

THE GOLD DIGGERS' SONG
(We're in the Money)

Music by HARRY WARREN
Lyrics by AL DUBIN

GOODY GOODY

Words by JOHNNY MERCER
Music by MATT MALNECK

GOOD MORNING STARSHINE
from the Broadway Musical Producion HAIR

Words by JAMES RADO and GEROME RAGNI
Music by GALT MacDERMOT

GREEN GREEN GRASS OF HOME

Words and Music by
CURLY PUTMAN

HAPPY TRAILS

from the Television Series THE ROY ROGERS SHOW

Words and Music by
DALE EVANS

Slow and tenderly

Some trails are hap-py ones, __ oth-ers are blue. It's the way you ride the trail that counts; __ here's a

HAPPY DAYS ARE HERE AGAIN

Words and Music by JACK YELLEN
and MILTON AGER

HIGH HOPES

Words by SAMMY CAHN
Music by JAMES VAN HEUSEN

Next time you're found _ with your chin on the ground, there's a
When trou-bles call _ and your back's to the wall, _ there's a

Instrumental

lot to be learned, _ so look a-round. _____
lot to be learned; _ that wall could fall. _____

Just what makes that lit-tle ol' ant _ think he'll move that rub-ber tree plant. _
Once there was a sil-ly ol' ram, _ thought he'd punch a hole in a dam. _

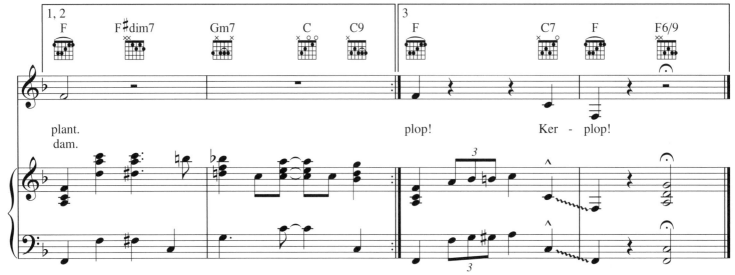

IF I ONLY HAD A BRAIN
from THE WIZARD OF OZ

Lyric by E.Y. "YIP" HARBURG
Music by HAROLD ARLEN

Scarecrow: Said a scare-crow swing-in' on a pole ___ to a black-bird sit-tin' on a
Tin Woodman: Said a tin-man rat-tlin' his ___ gibs ___ to a straw-man sad and wea-ry-
Cowardly Lion: Said a li-on poor neu-rot-ic lion, ___ to a miss who lis-tened to him

fence, ___ "Oh! the Lord gave me a soul, ___ but for-
eyed, ___ "Oh! the Lord gave me tin ribs, ___ but for-
rave, ___ "Oh! the Lord made me a li-on, but the

got to give me com - mon sense. ____ If I had an ounce of com - mon
got to put a heart in - side." ____ Then he banged his hol - low chest and
Lord for - got to make me brave." ____ Then his tail be - gan to curl and

Moderately

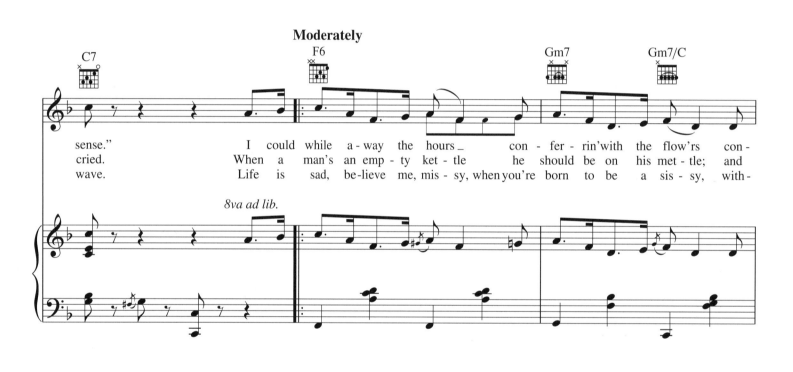

sense." I could while a - way the hours ___ con - fer - rin' with the flow'rs con -
cried. When a man's an emp - ty ket - tle he should be on his met - tle; and
wave. Life is sad, be - lieve me, mis - sy, when you're born to be a sis - sy, with -

sult - in' with the rain. _____ And my head I'd be scratch - in' while my
yet, I'm torn a - part _____ just be - cause I'm pre - sum - in' that I
out the vim and verve. _____ But I could change my hab - its, nev - er

I FEEL THE EARTH MOVE

Words and Music by
CAROLE KING

Ooh, __ dar -

I'D LIKE TO TEACH THE WORLD TO SING

Words and Music by BILL BACKER,
ROQUEL DAVIS, ROGER COOK
and ROGER GREENAWAY

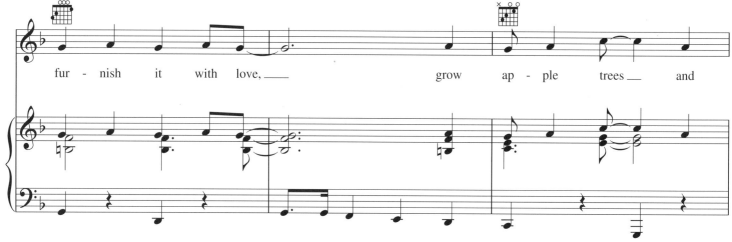

IT'S A SMALL WORLD

from Disneyland Resort® and Magic Kingdom® Park

Words and Music by RICHARD M. SHERMAN
and ROBERT B. SHERMAN

It's a world of laugh - ter, a
just of one moon and one

world of tears; it's a world of hopes and a
gold - en sun, and a smile means friend - ship to

JAMBALAYA
(On the Bayou)

Words and Music by
HANK WILLIAMS

JUMP

Words and Music by EDWARD VAN HALEN,
ALEX VAN HALEN and DAVID LEE ROTH

Jump!

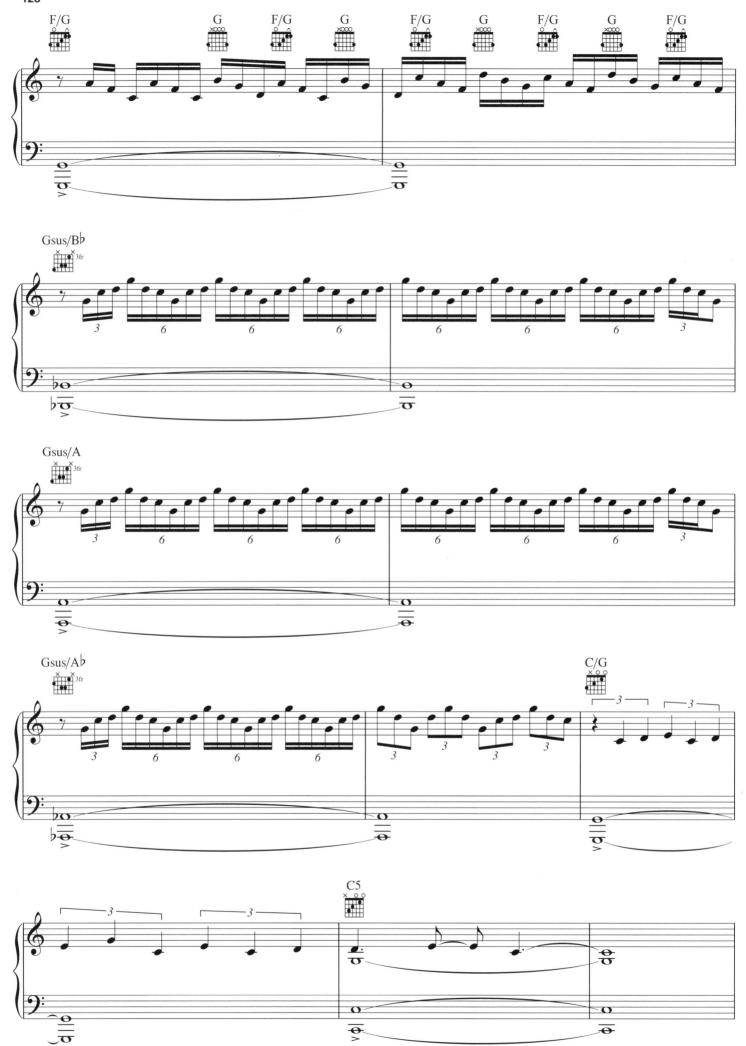

Might as well __ jump.

Vocal ad lib.

Go a-head and jump. __

Might as well __ jump.

Repeat and Fade

Optional Ending

8vb

JUMPING JACK FLASH

Words and Music by MICK JAGGER
and KEITH RICHARDS

Bluesy Rock

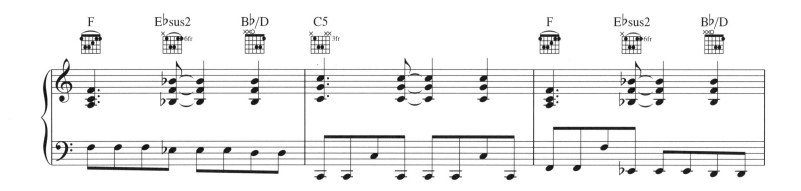

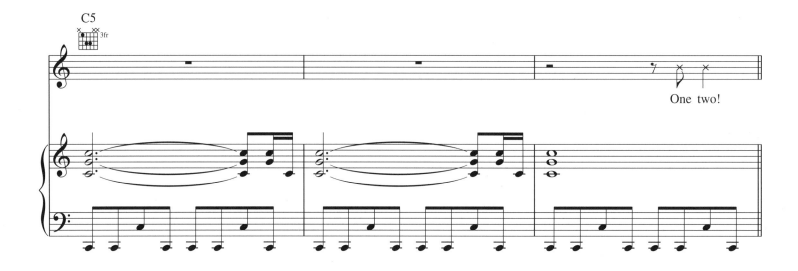

One two!

* Recorded a half step lower.

But it's al - right, I'm

Jump-ing Jack Flash, it's a gas, gas, gas.

To Coda

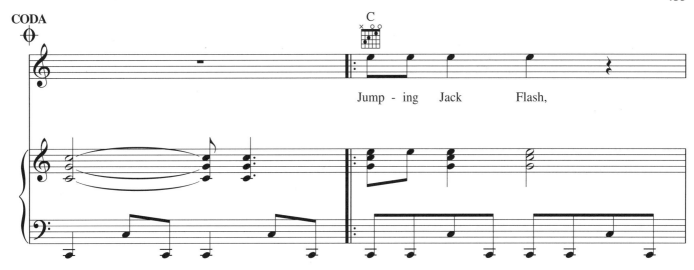

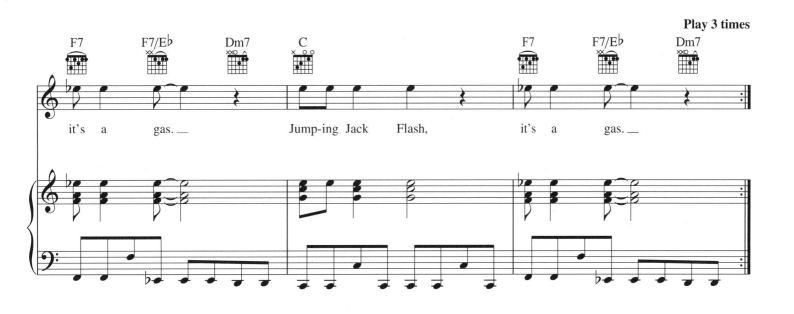

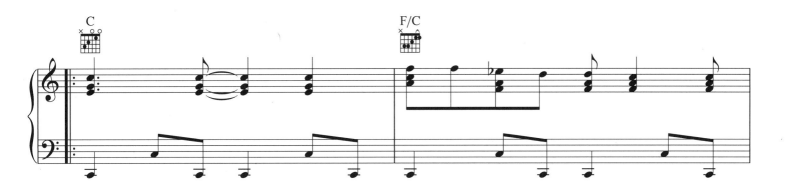

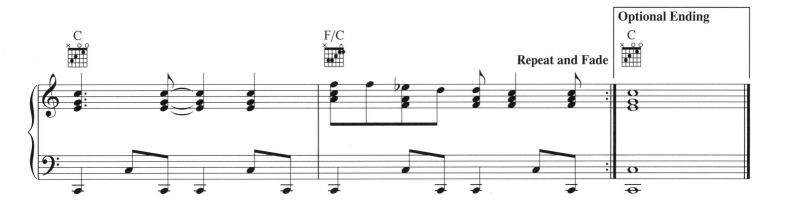

KEEP YOUR HANDS TO YOURSELF

Words and Music by
DANIEL BAIRD

Blues Rock

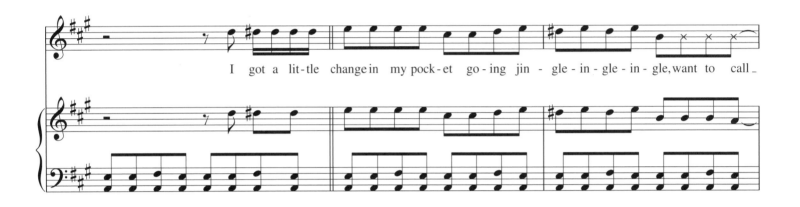

I got a lit-tle change in my pock-et go-ing jin - gle - in - gle - in - gle, want to call

___ you on the tel - e - phone, ba - by. I'll give you a ring. ___ But

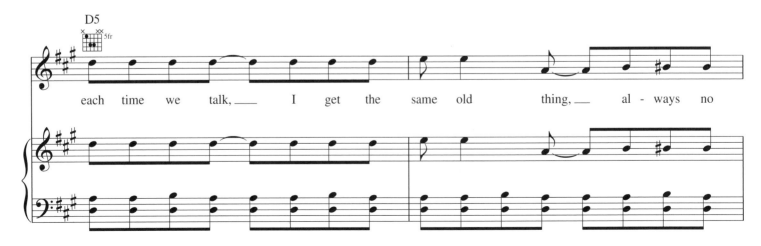

each time we talk, ___ I get the same old thing, ___ al - ways no

hug - ging, no kiss - ing un - til I get a _____ wed - ding ring. _____ My

hon - ey, my _____ ba - by, _____ don't put my love up - on no shelf. _____ She said, "Don't

give me no _____ lines, _____ and keep your hands to your - self." _____

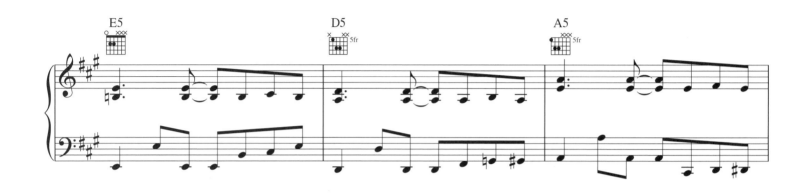

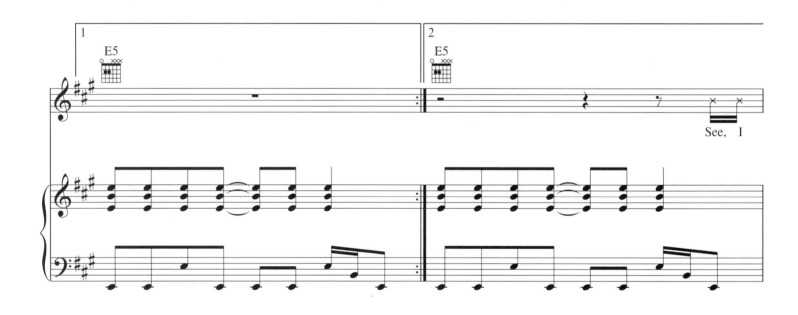

want-ed her real bad ___ and I was a - bout to give in, a that's when she

LET'S GET IT ON

Words and Music by MARVIN GAYE
and ED TOWNSEND

Slow Soul beat

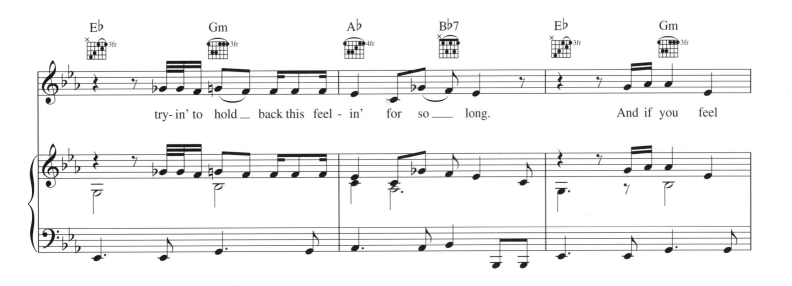

E♭ Gm A♭ B♭7 A♭
true. Oh, ba - by, ooh. Don't you know
E♭ Gm
how sweet and won - der - ful life can be? Ooh,
A♭ B♭7 A♭
ooh. I'm ask - in' you,
E♭ Gm
ba - by, to get it on with me. Ooh, ooh,

LET THE SUNSHINE IN
from the Broadway Musical Production HAIR

Words by JAMES RADO and GEROME RAGNI
Music by GALT MacDERMOT

We starve, look at one an-oth-er short of breath, walk-

-ing proud-ly in our win-ter coats, Wear - ing smells from lab-'ra-tor-ies,

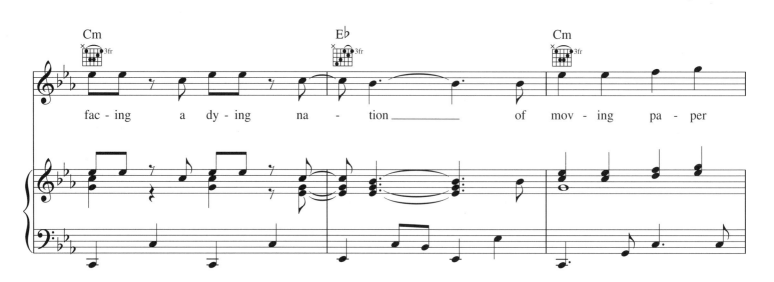

fac-ing a dy-ing na-tion _____ of mov-ing pa-per

LOVE FOR SALE

Words and Music by
COLE PORTER

MACK THE KNIFE
from THE THREEPENNY OPERA

English Words by MARC BLITZSTEIN
Original German Words by BERT BRECHT
Music by KURT WEILL

MARGARITAVILLE

Words and Music by
JIMMY BUFFETT

MR. BOJANGLES

Words and Music by
JERRY JEFF WALKER

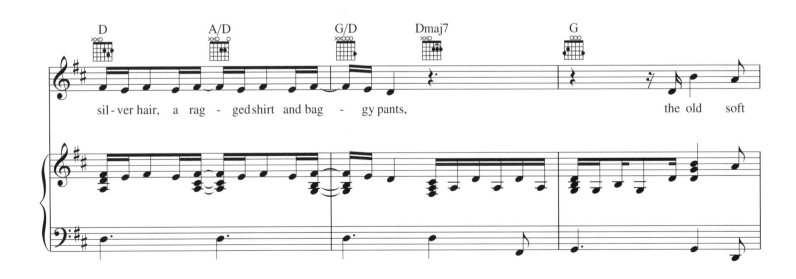

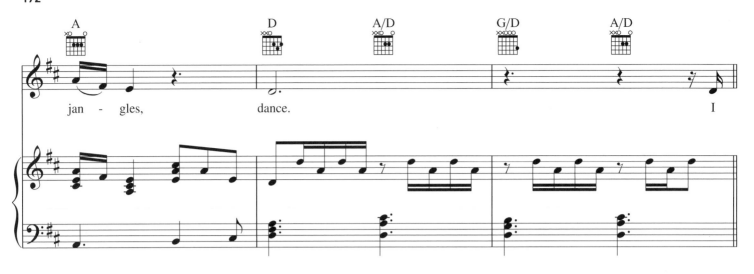

jan - gles,   dance.   I

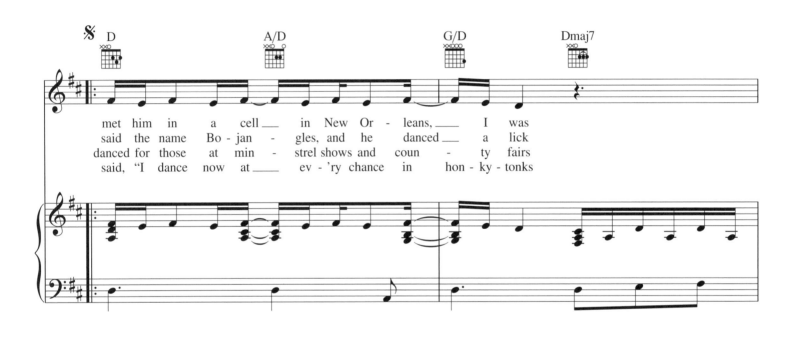

met him in a cell ___ in New Or - leans, ___ I was
said the name Bo - jan - gles, and he danced ___ a lick
danced for those at min - strel shows and coun - ty fairs
said, "I dance now at ___ ev - 'ry chance in hon - ky - tonks

down   and out. ___   He
a - cross   the cell. ___   He
through - out   the South. ___   He
for drinks   and tips. ___   But

MOONDANCE

Words and Music by
VAN MORRISON

MOUNTAIN MUSIC

Words and Music by
RANDY OWEN

THEME FROM "NEW YORK, NEW YORK"

from NEW YORK, NEW YORK

Words by FRED EBB
Music by JOHN KANDER

THE NIGHT THEY DROVE OLD DIXIE DOWN

Words and Music by
ROBBIE ROBERTSON

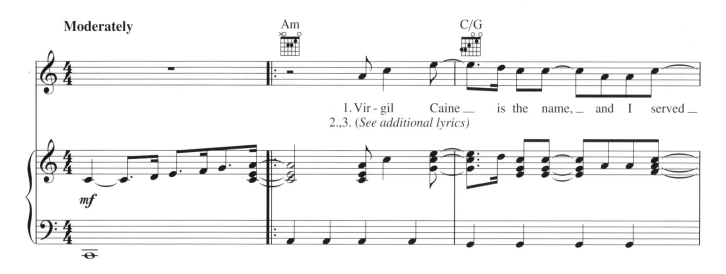

1. Vir - gil Caine __ is the name, __ and I served __
2.,3. (See additional lyrics)

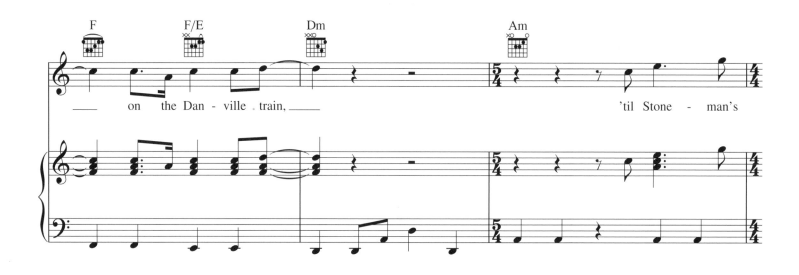

__ on the Dan - ville train, __ 'til Stone - man's

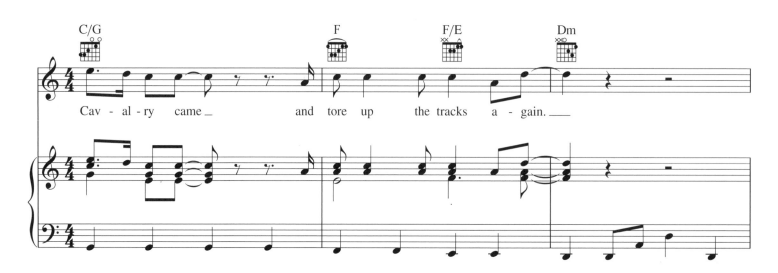

Cav - al - ry came __ and tore up the tracks a - gain. __

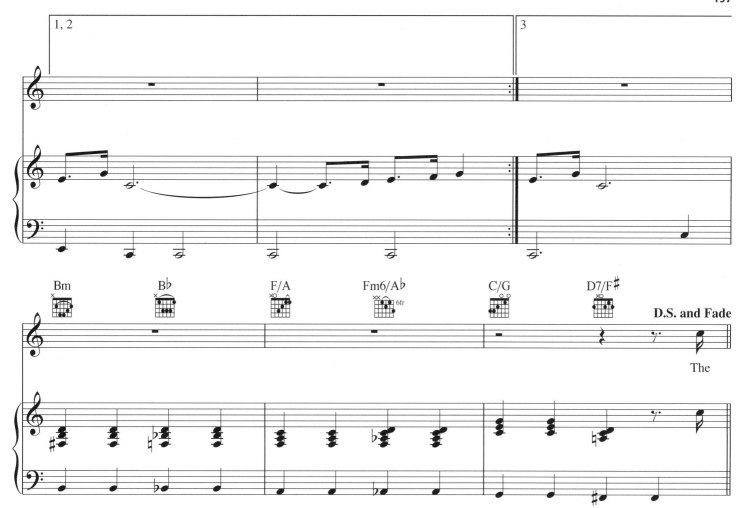

Additional Lyrics

2. Back with my wife in Tennessee
   When one day she called to me,
   "Virgil, quick, come see:
   There goes Robert E. Lee!"
   Now, I don't mind choppin' wood
   And I don't care if the money's no good,
   Ya take what ya need and ya leave the rest
   But they should never have taken
   The very best.
   (Repeat Chorus)

3. Like my father before me,
   I will work the land.
   And like my brother above me
   Who took a rebel stand.
   He was just eighteen, proud and brave,
   But a Yankee laid him in his grave.
   I swear by the mud below my feet,
   You can't raise a Caine back up
   When he's in defeat.
   (Repeat Chorus with final ending)

OVER THE RAINBOW

from THE WIZARD OF OZ

Music by HAROLD ARLEN
Lyric by E.Y. "YIP" HARBURG

SHE LOVES YOU

Words and Music by JOHN LENNON
and PAUL McCARTNEY

Moderately

She loves you, yeah, yeah, yeah. __ She loves you, yeah,

yeah, yeah. __ She loves you, yeah, yeah, yeah,

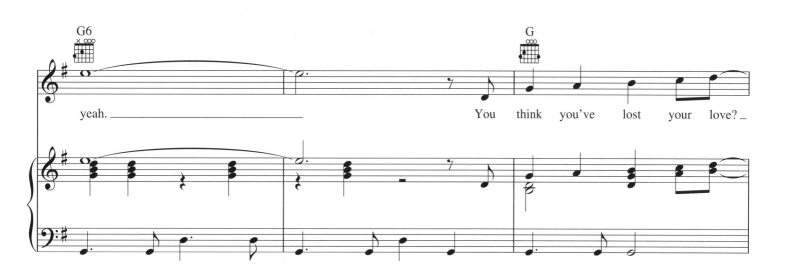

yeah. _____ You think you've lost your love? __

PARTY IN THE U.S.A.

Words and Music by JESSICA CORNISH,
LUKASZ GOTTWALD and CLAUDE KELLY

Moderate Pop

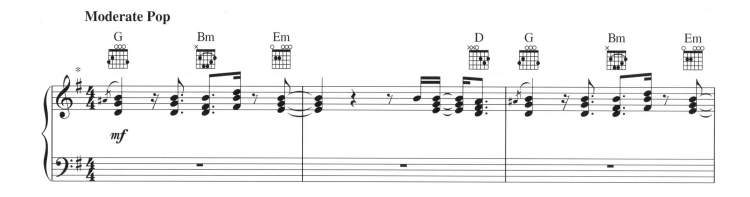

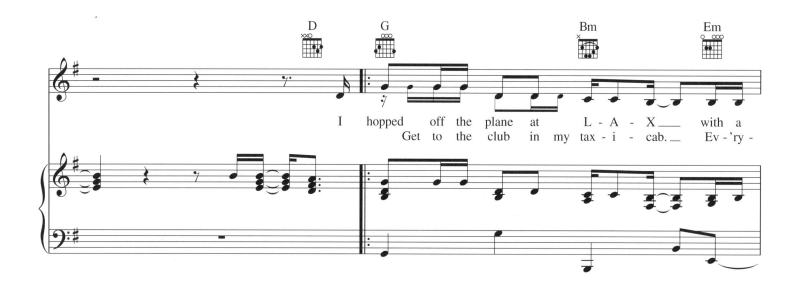

I hopped off the plane at L - A - X___ with a
Get to the club in my tax-i-cab.___ Ev - 'ry-

dream and my car-di-gan.___ Wel-come to the land of fame, ex-cess.___ She's
bod-y's look-in' at me now,___ like, "Who's that chick that's rock-in' kicks?___ She's

* Recorded a half step lower.

RHINESTONE COWBOY

Words and Music by
LARRY WEISS

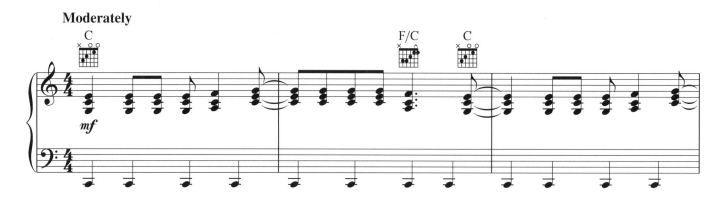

I've been walk-ing these streets __ so long, __ and a
Well, I real-ly don't mind __ the rain, __

sing-ing the same old song. I know ev-'ry crack on these dir-
smile __ can hide the pain, but you're down when you're rid-ing a train __

SINGIN' IN THE RAIN

from SINGIN' IN THE RAIN

Lyric by ARTHUR FREED
Music by NACIO HERB BROWN

SUMMERTIME BLUES

Words and Music by EDDIE COCHRAN
and JERRY CAPEHART

Some - times I won - der what I'm a - gon - na do, __ but there ain't no cure for the

Play 3 times

sum - mer - time __ blues.

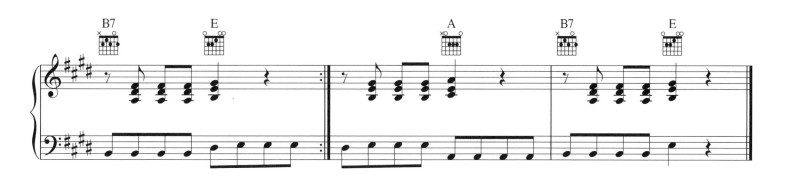

SOMETHIN' STUPID

Words and Music by
C. CARSON PARKS

SUMMER WIND

English Words by JOHNNY MERCER
Original German Lyrics by HANS BRADTKE
Music by HENRY MAYER

SUNSHINE OF YOUR LOVE

Words and Music by JACK BRUCE,
PETE BROWN and ERIC CLAPTON

SWAYIN' TO THE MUSIC
(Slow Dancin')

Words and Music by
JACK TEMPCHIN

TAKE IT EASY

Words and Music by JACKSON BROWNE
and GLENN FREY

SWEET GEORGIA BROWN

Words and Music by BEN BERNIE,
MACEO PINKARD and KENNETH CASEY

TEQUILA SUNRISE

Words and Music by DON HENLEY
and GLENN FREY

It's an-oth-er te-qui - la sun - rise

star - in' slow - ly 'cross ___ the sky, ___

C
Em
C
sun goes down, just an - oth - er lone - ly boy in town,
Em
Am
D7
and she's out run - nin' 'round.
G/D
G
She was - n't just an - oth - er wom - an
D
Am
and I could - n't keep from com - in' on,

Take an-oth-er shot of cour - age,

won - der why the right words nev - er come, _____

_____ you just get numb. _____

THAT'S WHAT FRIENDS ARE FOR

Music by BURT BACHARACH
Words by CAROLE BAYER SAGER

VOLARE

Music by DOMENICO MODUGNO
Original Italian Text by D. MODUGNO and F. MIGLIACCI
English Lyric by MITCHELL PARISH

Some-times the world is a val-ley of heart-aches and tears,
Pen-so che un so-gno co-sì non ri-tor-ni mai più:

and in the hus-tle and bus-tle no sun-shine ap-
mi di-pin-ge-vo le ma-ni e la fac-cia di

TIP-TOE THRU' THE TULIPS WITH ME

Words by AL DUBIN
Music by JOE BURKE

WHAT I GOT

Words and Music by BRAD NOWELL,
ERIC WILSON, FLOYD GAUGH
and LINDON ROBERTS

YOU CAN LEAVE YOUR HAT ON

Words and Music by
RANDY NEWMAN

Moderately

Ba - by, take off your coat _____ real _____ slow.

WILD NIGHT

Words and Music by
VAN MORRISON

Moderate Rock

N.C.

f

Male: As you brush your shoes, you stand be-fore __ your mir-

ror. And you comb your hair,

grab your coat and hat. *Female:* And __ you walk __

* Female vocal written one octave higher than sung.

girls walk by dressed up for ___ each oth - er.

And the boys do the boo - gie woo - gie on the cor - ner of the

street. _____ *Female:* And the peo - ple pass - ing by

just stare in wild ___ won - der, ___ yeah. And in -

side the juke - box roars ___ just ___ like thun - der.

D.S. al Coda

CODA

Male: Wild _____ night _ is call -

Ooh, _____ ooh _____ wee, ___

wild ___ night ___ is call - ing.

Ooh, _____ ooh _____ wee, ___

the wild ___ night ___ is call - ing.

THE GRAMMY AWARDS

SONGBOOKS FROM HAL LEONARD

These elite collections of the nominees and winners of
Grammy Awards since the honor's inception in 1958
provide a snapshot of the changing times in popular music.

PIANO/VOCAL/GUITAR

GRAMMY AWARDS RECORD OF THE YEAR 1958-2011
Beat It • Beautiful Day • Bridge over Troubled Water • Don't Know Why • Don't Worry, Be Happy • The Girl from Ipanema (Garôta De Ipanema) • Hotel California • I Will Always Love You • Just the Way You Are • Mack the Knife • Moon River • My Heart Will Go on (Love Theme from 'Titanic') • Rehab • Sailing • Unforgettable • Up, Up and Away • The Wind Beneath My Wings • and more.
00313603 P/V/G...$19.99

THE GRAMMY AWARDS SONG OF THE YEAR 1958-1969
Battle of New Orleans • Born Free • Fever • The Good Life • A Hard Day's Night • Harper Valley P.T.A. • Hello, Dolly! • Hey Jude • King of the Road • Little Green Apples • Mrs. Robinson • Ode to Billy Joe • People • Somewhere, My Love • Strangers in the Night • A Time for Us (Love Theme) • Volare • Witchcraft • Yesterday • and more.
00313598 P/V/G...$19.99

THE GRAMMY AWARDS SONG OF THE YEAR 1970-1979
Alone Again (Naturally) • American Pie • At Seventeen • Don't It Make My Brown Eyes Blue • Honesty • (I Never Promised You A) Rose Garden • I Write the Songs • Killing Me Softly with His Song • Let It Be • Me and Bobby McGee • Send in the Clowns • Song Sung Blue • Stayin' Alive • Three Times a Lady • The Way We Were • You're So Vain • You've Got a Friend • and more.
00313599 P/V/G...$19.99

THE GRAMMY AWARDS SONG OF THE YEAR 1980-1989
Against All Odds (Take a Look at Me Now) • Always on My Mind • Beat It • Bette Davis Eyes • Don't Worry, Be Happy • Ebony and Ivory • Endless Love • Every Breath You Take • Eye of the Tiger • Fame • Fast Car • Hello • I Just Called to Say I Love You • La Bamba • Nine to Five • The Rose • Somewhere Out There • Time After Time • We Are the World • and more.
00313600 P/V/G...$19.99

THE GRAMMY AWARDS SONG OF THE YEAR 1990-1999
Can You Feel the Love Tonight • (Everything I Do) I Do It for You • From a Distance • Give Me One Reason • I Swear • Kiss from a Rose • Losing My Religion • My Heart Will Go on (Love Theme from 'Titanic') • Nothing Compares 2 U • Smooth • Streets of Philadelphia • Tears in Heaven • Unforgettable • Walking in Memphis • A Whole New World • You Oughta Know • and more.
00313601 P/V/G...$19.99

THE GRAMMY AWARDS SONG OF THE YEAR 2000-2009
Beautiful • Beautiful Day • Breathe • Chasing Pavements • Complicated • Dance with My Father • Daughters • Don't Know Why • Fallin' • I Hope You Dance • I'm Yours • Live like You Were Dying • Poker Face • Rehab • Single Ladies (Put a Ring on It) • A Thousand Miles • Umbrella • Use Somebody • Viva La Vida • and more.
00313602 P/V/G...$19.99

THE GRAMMY AWARDS BEST COUNTRY SONG 1964-2011
Always on My Mind • Before He Cheats • Behind Closed Doors • Bless the Broken Road • Butterfly Kisses • Dang Me • Forever and Ever, Amen • The Gambler • I Still Believe in You • I Swear • King of the Road • Live like You Were Dying • Love Can Build a Bridge • Need You Now • On the Road Again • White Horse • You Decorated My Life • and more.
00313604 P/V/G...$19.99

THE GRAMMY AWARDS BEST R&B SONG 1958-2011
After the Love Has Gone • Ain't No Sunshine • Be Without You • Billie Jean • End of the Road • Good Golly Miss Molly • Hit the Road Jack • If You Don't Know Me by Now • Papa's Got a Brand New Bag • Respect • Shine • Single Ladies (Put a Ring on It) • (Sittin' On) the Dock of the Bay • Superstition • U Can't Touch This • We Belong Together • and more.
00313605 P/V/G...$19.99

THE GRAMMY AWARDS BEST POP & ROCK GOSPEL ALBUMS (2000-2011)
Call My Name • Come on Back to Me • Deeper Walk • Forever • Gone • I Need You • I Smile • I Will Follow • King • Leaving 99 • Lifesong • Looking Back at You • Much of You • My Love Remains • Say So • Somebody's Watching • Step by Step/Forever We Will Sing • Tunnel • Unforgetful You • You Hold My World • Your Love Is a Song • and more.
00313680 P/V/G...$16.99

ELECTRONIC KEYBOARD

THE GRAMMY AWARDS RECORD OF THE YEAR 1958-2011 – VOL. 160
All I Wanna Do • Bridge over Troubled Water • Don't Know Why • The Girl from Ipanema (Garôta De Ipanema) • Hotel California • I Will Always Love You • Just the Way You Are • Killing Me Softly with His Song • Love Will Keep Us Together • Rehab • Unforgettable • What's Love Got to Do with It • The Wind Beneath My Wings • and more.
00100315 E-Z Play Today #160 ....$16.99

PRO VOCAL
WOMEN'S EDITIONS

THE GRAMMY AWARDS BEST FEMALE POP VOCAL PERFORMANCE 1990-1999 — VOL. 57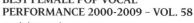
Book/CD Pack
All I Wanna Do • Building a Mystery • Constant Craving • I Will Always Love You • I Will Remember You • My Heart Will Go on (Love Theme from 'Titanic') • No More "I Love You's" • Something to Talk About (Let's Give Them Something to Talk About) • Unbreak My Heart • Vision of Love.
00740446 Melody/Lyrics/Chords.................$14.99

THE GRAMMY AWARDS BEST FEMALE POP VOCAL PERFORMANCE 2000-2009 – VOL. 58
Book/CD Pack
Ain't No Other Man • Beautiful • Chasing Pavements • Don't Know Why • Halo • I Try • I'm like a Bird • Rehab • Since U Been Gone • Sunrise.
00740447 Melody/Lyrics/Chords.................$14.99

MEN'S EDITIONS

THE GRAMMY AWARDS BEST MALE POP VOCAL PERFORMANCE 1990-1999 – VOL. 59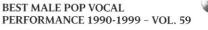
Book/CD Pack
Brand New Day • Can You Feel the Love Tonight • Candle in the Wind 1997 • Change the World • If I Ever Lose My Faith in You • Kiss from a Rose • My Father's Eyes • Oh, Pretty Woman • Tears in Heaven • When a Man Loves a Woman.
00740448 Melody/Lyrics/Chords.................$14.99

THE GRAMMY AWARDS BEST MALE POP VOCAL PERFORMANCE 2000-2009 – VOL. 60
Book/CD Pack
Cry Me a River • Daughters • Don't Let Me Be Lonely Tonight • Make It Mine • Say • Waiting on the World to Change • What Goes Around...Comes Around Interlude • Your Body Is a Wonderland.
00740449 Melody/Lyrics/Chords.................$14.99

Prices, contents, and availabilbity subject to change without notice.

HAL•LEONARD® CORPORATION
7777 W. Bluemound Rd. P.O. Box 13819 Milwaukee, WI 53213

www.halleonard.com